CAN I BECOME A ____ BECAUSE I LIKE ____?

CAREERS FOR KIDS BY SUBJECTS

CHILDREN'S JOBS & CAREERS REFERENCE BOOKS

Speedy Publishing LLC

40 E. Main St. #1156

Newark, DE 19711

www.speedypublishing.com

Copyright 2018

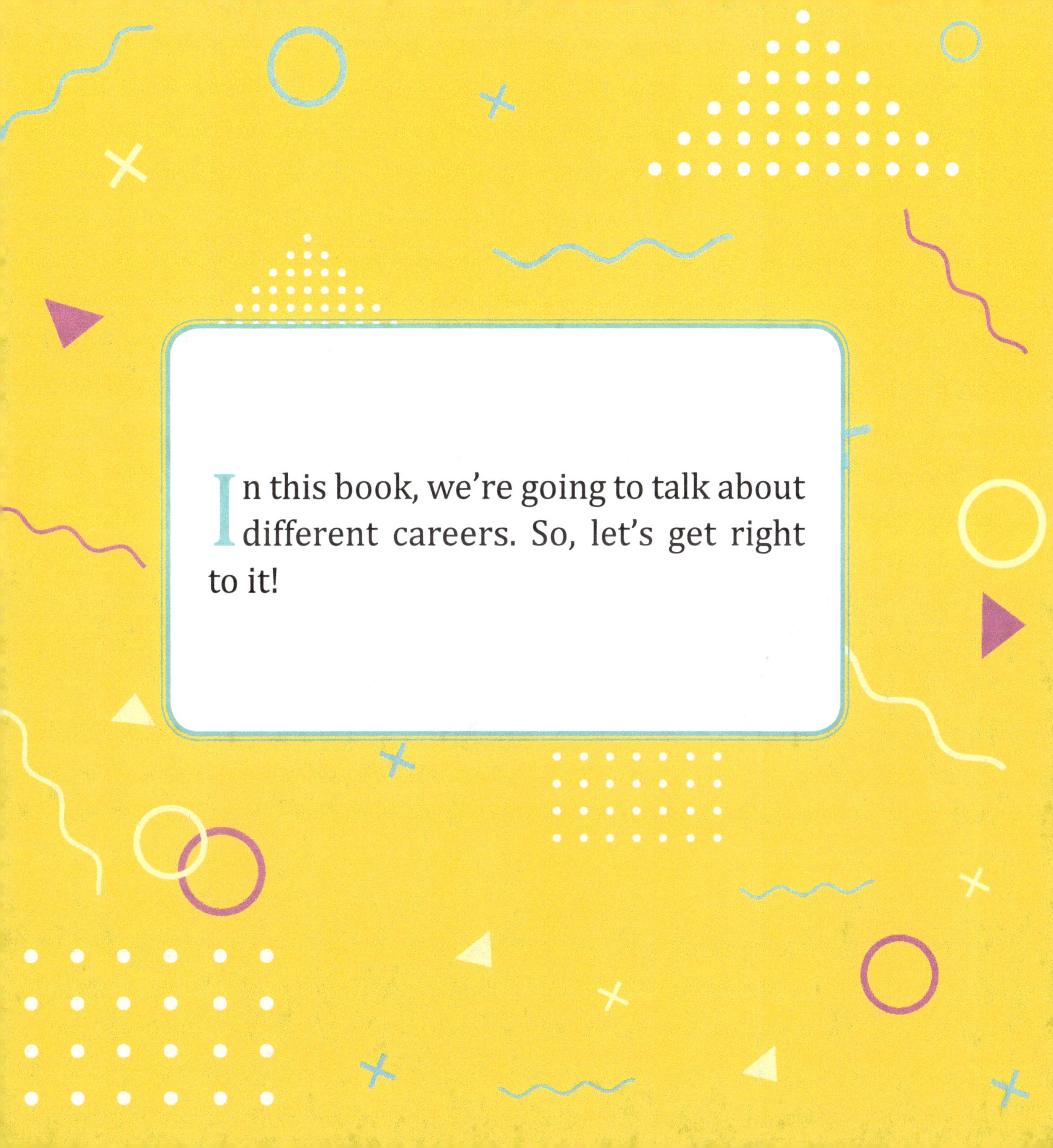
In this book, we're going to talk about different careers. So, let's get right to it!

CAREER

Years ago, people would stay in the same careers for most of their lives. However, that has been gradually changing over the past 30 years. By the time you are finished with school and you are ready to start your career life, there may be jobs that don't even exist today! If you have lots of different skills, you can keep re-inventing yourself as you get older and you discover new interests and talents.

Here are some of the up-and-coming careers to help you think about what you like best and which career or careers might be best for your talents and skills. If you don't like any of these, there are also lots of other careers you can research on your own. Another option is to start your own business and create a role for yourself as an entrepreneur!

TEACHER ASKING HER STUDENTS A QUESTION

ELEMENTARY SCHOOL TEACHERS

If you like children and you're interested in lots of different subjects, you may want to become an elementary school teacher. By 2024, there will be more than 75,000 new positions for general elementary school teachers in the United States with a median annual salary of over $50,000. To be an elementary school teacher, you'll need to have at least a bachelor's degree.

ELEMENTARY SCHOOL KIDS AND TEACHER HAVING A DISCUSSION

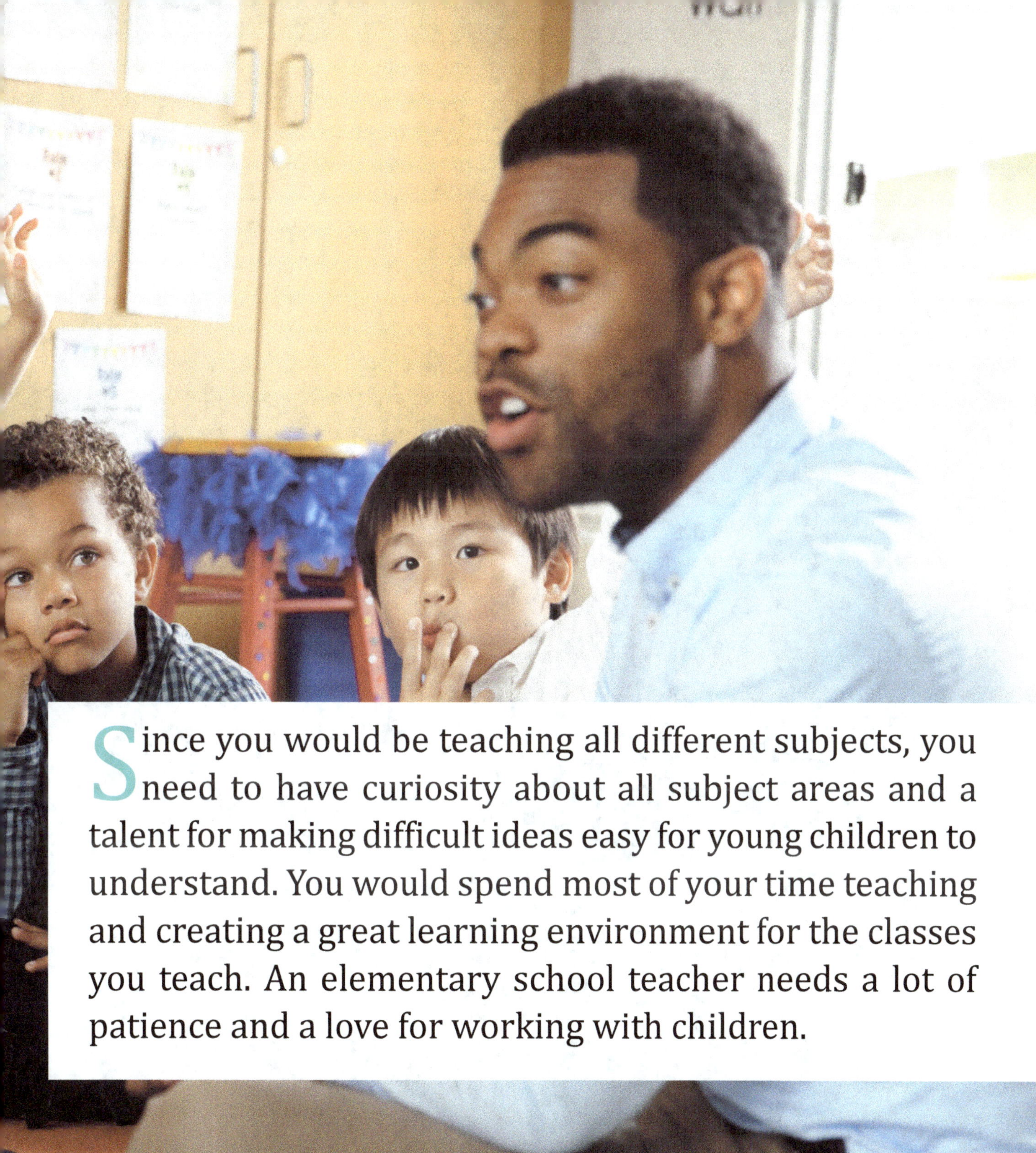

Since you would be teaching all different subjects, you need to have curiosity about all subject areas and a talent for making difficult ideas easy for young children to understand. You would spend most of your time teaching and creating a great learning environment for the classes you teach. An elementary school teacher needs a lot of patience and a love for working with children.

NURSE EXAMINING LITTLE GIRL WITH STETHOSCOPE

NURSE PRACTITIONERS

If you enjoy helping to make sick people well, then nursing may be a great career for you. By 2024, there will be at least 40,000 new positions created for nurses with a median annual salary of $95,000. As a nurse, you would be supporting the work of physicians as they diagnose patients and treat their illnesses.

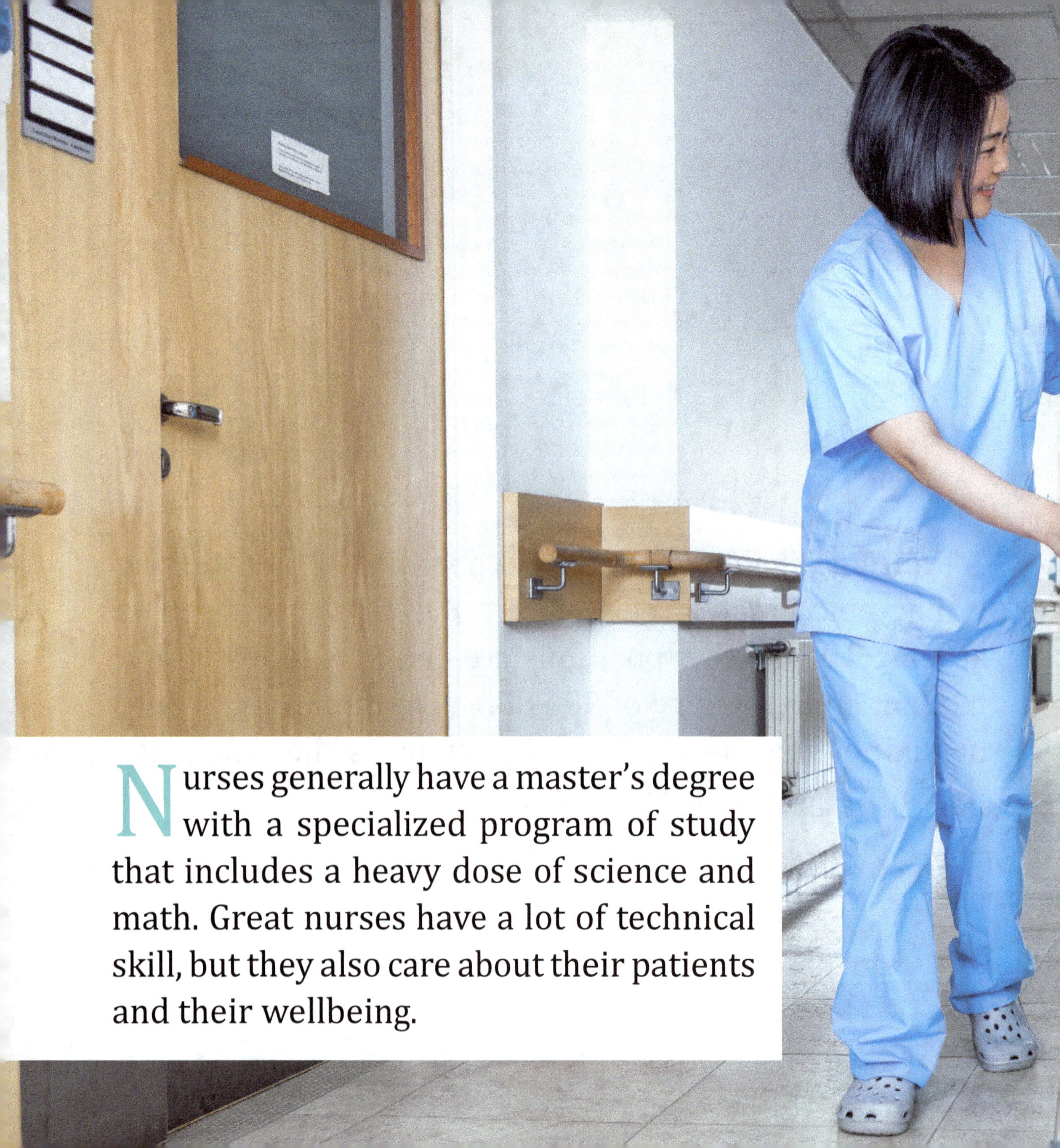

Nurses generally have a master's degree with a specialized program of study that includes a heavy dose of science and math. Great nurses have a lot of technical skill, but they also care about their patients and their wellbeing.

SENIOR PATIENT BEING ASSISTED BY A NURSE

FINANCIAL MANAGERS

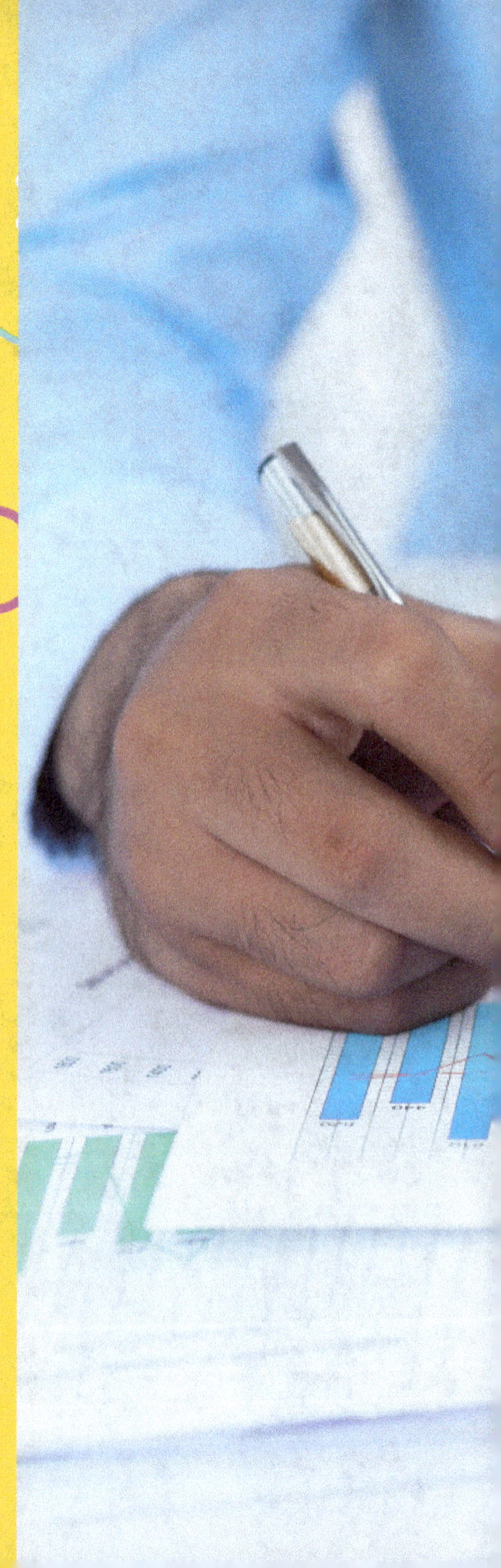

If you enjoy numbers, banking, and accounting and are good at practical math, you may want to consider a career as a financial manager. Every organization small or large needs someone to manage a department that deals with the financial planning of that organization.

FINANCIAL MANAGER ANALYZING CHARTS AND GRAPHS

FINANCIAL MANAGER REVIEWING DATA IN FINANCIAL CHARTS AND GRAPHS

Depending on the level of the position, you might need special training as a certified public accountant. It's projected that there will be over 35,000 new positions for financial managers by 2024.

They receive significant salaries of over $100,000 a year or more. Their roles and responsibilities include directing the financial activities for their organization, such as budgeting, accounting, and financial planning. You

need at least a bachelor's degree to become a financial planner and it's essential that you understand the ins and outs of bookkeeping.

ELECTRICIAN FATHER AND HELPING SON READY FOR WORK

ELECTRICIANS

If you are fascinated by electrical motors and always wondered about how electricity works, you may want to pursue a career as an electrician. There will be more than 86,000 new positions in the United States for electricians by 2024. Their median annual salary is about $50,000.

Their chief role is to install as well as maintain and repair appliances and equipment that are powered by electricity. They troubleshoot electrical problems and add

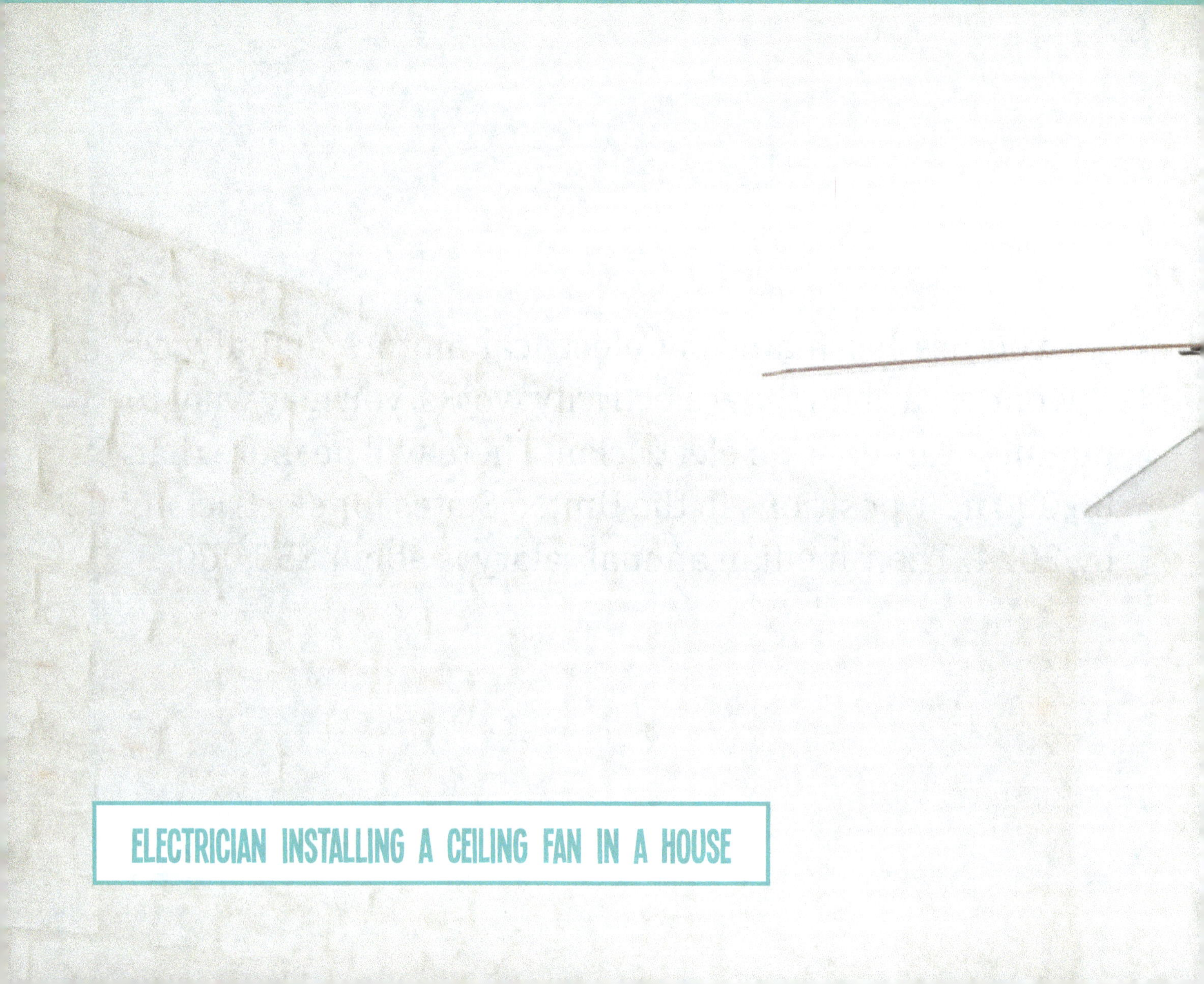

ELECTRICIAN INSTALLING A CEILING FAN IN A HOUSE

new electrical lines in homes and offices too. To become an electrician, you need at least a high-school diploma.

ELECTRICIAN

Most electricians have at least a two-year technical degree. You need to have a strong interest in science as well as mechanical ability to become an electrician. It is a potentially dangerous job so you must be methodical and careful when you work.

LAWYERS

Do you excel at reading, writing, and studying? Are you interested in legal agreements and how laws are enforced? Do you find history interesting? If so, you may want to pursue a career as a lawyer. There are many different types of lawyers and by 2024, it's projected that there will be more than 40,000 new positions for this profession. Lawyers are paid very well. Most lawyers have a median annual salary of over $110,000.

LAWYER IN THE LAW LIBRARY AT A UNIVERSITY

Their major role is to represent their clients in both civil and criminal cases. It takes quite a bit of specialized training to become a lawyer and you need four years of undergraduate work, plus three years in law school, so that's seven years of study after graduating from high school. Not all lawyers represent clients in court, but those who do must be excellent, persuasive speakers.

LAWYER MAKING A CLOSING STATEMENT IN THE COURT ROOM

WHOLESALE AND MANUFACTURING SALES REPRESENTATIVES

Are you interested in representing products and selling them to customers and businesses? Do you enjoy being of service to other people? If so, you may want to consider becoming a sales representative. Almost every company that sells products and services needs sales representatives.

CUSTOMER GETS ADVICE FROM SALESWOMAN WHILE SHOPPING

In fact, it's estimated that by 2024, there will be more than 90,000 new positions available for people who want this career. The median annual salary is $55,000 and there are sometimes bonuses for those sales people who excel in their field.

SALESPERSON SELLING CARS AT DEALERSHIP TO BUYER

As a sales representative your major role would be to sell products and services for companies who manufacture those items or for wholesalers who want to resell them. You have to be a "people person" who really enjoys others to do this job well.

SALESWOMAN SHOWING CUSTOMER INFORMATION FROM CATALOG

SOFTWARE DEVELOPER WORKING ON COMPUTER AT THE OFFICE

SOFTWARE SYSTEM DEVELOPERS

Are you interested in computers? Do you find it easy to learn how to code and understand different computer languages? Are you fascinated by software applications and how they work? If so, you may want to consider a career as a software system developer.

By 2024, there will be more than 50,000 new positions in this field. This is a lucrative field and the median annual salary is $100,000. Software system developers create new types of operating systems for computers.

PROGRAMMER TYPING DATA CODE

PROGRAMMER WORKING IN A SOFTWARE DEVELOPMENT COMPANY

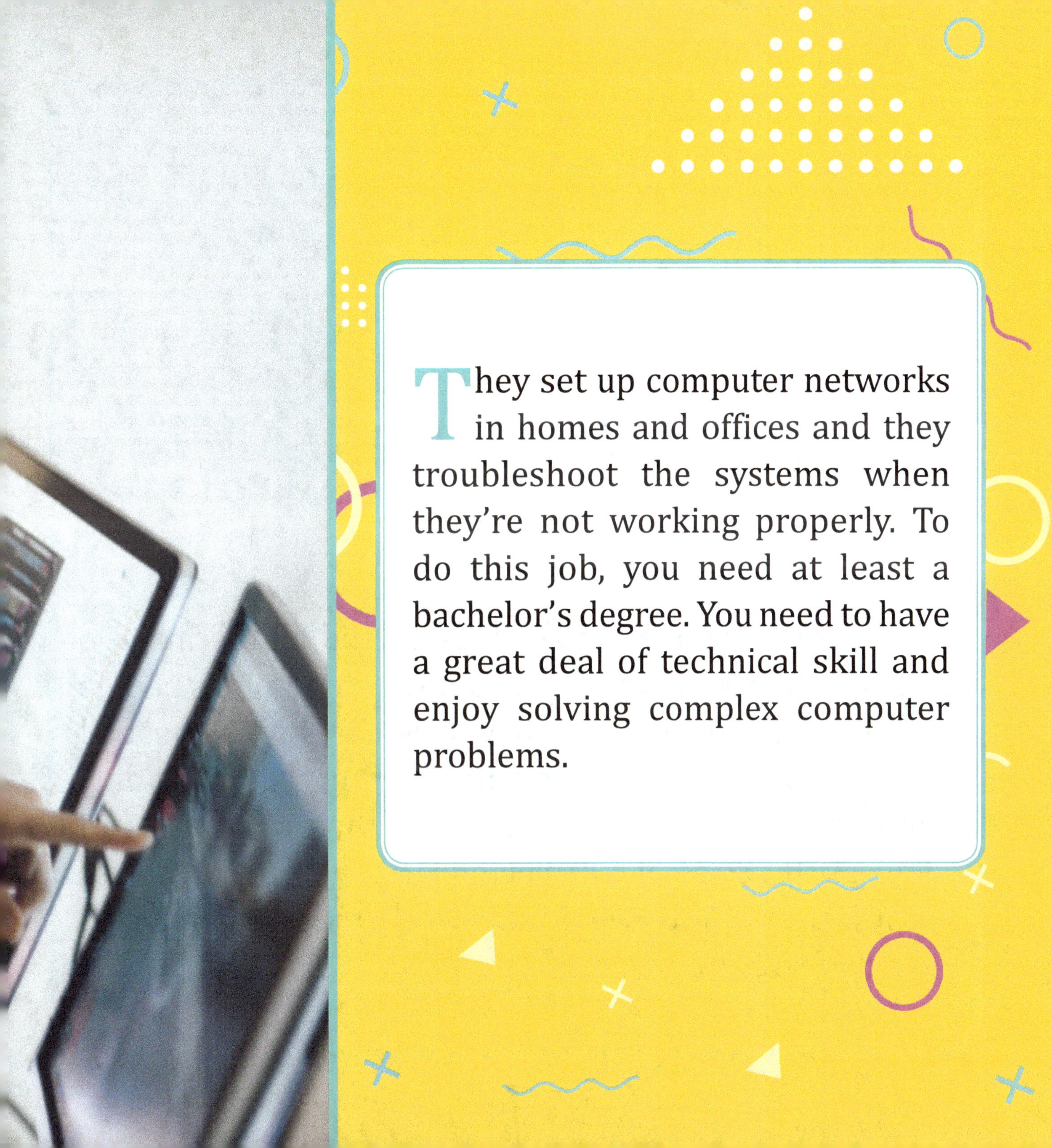They set up computer networks in homes and offices and they troubleshoot the systems when they're not working properly. To do this job, you need at least a bachelor's degree. You need to have a great deal of technical skill and enjoy solving complex computer problems.

MARKET RESEARCH ANALYSTS AND MARKETING SPECIALISTS

Are you interested in advertising and marketing? Do you enjoy research to find out which products people are interested in and why they decide to buy? Almost all companies need assistance with their marketing so they can attract new customers and sell their products and services. By 2024, it's projected that there will be over 90,000 new positions in this field with the median annual salary of $62,000.

MARKETING ANALYST WORKING IN CAFE

In this career, your role would be to analyze the market conditions for the company you work for and to create innovative campaigns so customers will take notice and buy your company's products. You need at least a

bachelor's degree to do this job and an understanding of traditional marketing techniques as well as how to use social media as a marketing tool.

PHYSICAL THERAPISTS

Do you enjoy helping other people get in better physical shape so they can be healthier? Like nurses and physicians, physical therapists work in the health field. As the population ages in the United States, there are an increasing number of positions in health fields.

PATIENT BEING ASSISTED BY PHYSICAL THERAPIST

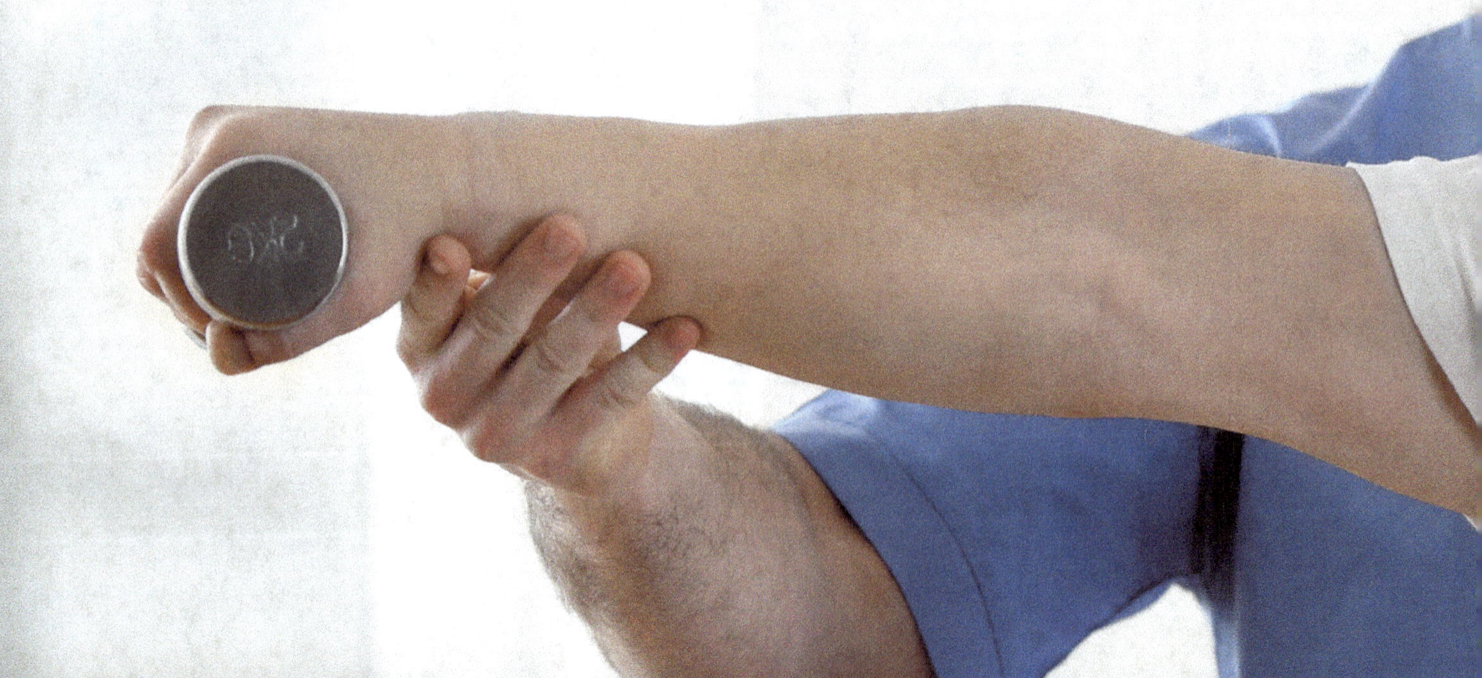

PHYSICAL THERAPIST WORKING WITH ELDERLY PATIENT IN A CLINIC

would help your patients do the proper exercises so they can recover from injuries or alleviate the chronic suffering they have due to illnesses.

You'll need a specialized professional degree to be a physical therapist. If you have a genuine desire to help people and a lot of patience when their recovery is slow then you may be well suited for this career.

PHYSICAL THERAPIST HELPING PATIENT TO WALK

DOCTOR AND PATIENT

PHYSICIANS AND SURGEONS

Have you always wanted to heal people from their illnesses? Do you have science ability and the desire to study for many years to become skillful as a doctor or surgeon? By the year 2024, there will be more than 50,000 new positions for physicians in all types of specialized fields. Doctors, especially surgeons, earn a median annual salary of $190,000 or more.

They have to attain doctoral degrees and go through a long course of study for their area of specialty. A doctor has to study for four years in medical school and then has to go through residency training for three to seven years before getting a medical license. If you have the desire to save lives with your surgical skills then you should consider this important career.

PHYSICIAN

WHAT CAREER WILL YOU CHOOSE?

By the time you are ready to start your first career, there may be new careers that are not available now. Pay attention to the things you enjoy in school and the hobbies that you love. You will probably change careers as many as eight different times or more during your lifetime and each time you can highlight the talents you can contribute and find out which things you love to do.

Awesome! Now that you've learned about different careers you may want to read more about some famous entrepreneurs in the Baby Professor book The Most Famous Entrepreneurs of All Time - Biography Book 3rd Grade | Children's Biographies.

E
E
R

Visit
BABY PROFESSOR
EDUCATION KIDS
www.BabyProfessorBooks.com
to download Free Baby Professor eBooks
and view our catalog of new and exciting
Children's Books

9 798886 943664 1